女　　神
THE GODDESSES

郭沫若　著

勒斯特
巴恩斯　译

Written by Guo Moruo

Translated by Jong Lester and A.C. Barnes

外文出版社
FOREIGN LANGUAGES PRESS

图书在版编目(CIP)数据

女神:汉英对照/郭沫若著.—北京:外文出版社,2001
(经典的回声)
ISBN 7 – 119 – 02778 – 6

Ⅰ.女... Ⅱ.郭... Ⅲ.英语 – 对照读物,诗歌 – 汉、
英 Ⅳ.H319.4:I

中国版本图书馆 CIP 数据核字(2000)第 78568 号

外文出版社网址:
http://www.flp.com.cn
外文出版社电子信箱:
info@flp.com.cn
sales@flp.com.cn

经典的回声

女 神(汉英对照)

作 者	郭沫若	
译 者	勒斯特 巴恩斯	
责任编辑	刘春英 刘新航	
封面设计	陈 军	
出版发行	外文出版社	
社 址	北京市百万庄大街 24 号	邮政编码 100037
电 话	(010) 68320579(总编室）	
	(010) 68329514/68327211(推广发行部)	
印 刷	北京市铁成印刷厂	
经 销	新华书店/外文书店	
开 本	大 32 开(850×1168)毫米 字 数 94 千字	
印 数	8001 – 11000 册 印 张 6.125	
版 次	2003 年 3 月第 1 版第 2 次印刷	
装 别	平 装	
书 号	ISBN 7 – 119 – 02778 – 6/I.448(外)	
定 价	11.00 元	

出 版 前 言

　　本社专事外文图书的编辑出版,几十年来用英文翻译出版了大量的中国文学作品和文化典籍,上自先秦,下迄现当代,力求全面而准确地反映中国文学及中国文化的基本面貌和灿烂成就。这些英译图书均取自相关领域著名的、权威的作品,英译则出自国内外译界名家。每本图书的编选、翻译过程均极其审慎严肃,精雕细琢,中文作品及相应的英译版本均堪称经典。

　　我们意识到,这些英译精品,不单有对外译介的意义,而且对国内英文学习者、爱好者及英译工作者,也是极有价值的读本。为此,我们对这些英译精品做了认真的遴选,编排成汉英对照的形式,陆续推出,以飨读者。

外文出版社

Publisher's Note

Foreign Languages Press is dedicated to the editing, translating and publishing of books in foreign languages. Over the past several decades it has published, in English, a great number of China's classics and records as well as literary works from the Qin down to modern times, in the aim to fully display the best part of the Chinese culture and its achievements. These books in the original are famous and authoritative in their respective fields, and their English translations are masterworks produced by notable translators both at home and abroad. Each book is carefully compiled and translated with minute precision. Consequently, the English versions as well as their Chinese originals may both be rated as classics.

It is generally considered that these English translations are not only significant for introducing China to the outside world but also useful reading materials for domestic English learners and translators. For this reason, we have carefully selected some of these books, and will publish them successively in Chinese-English bilingual form.

Foreign Languages Press

目 录
CONTENTS

郭沫若像

The picture of Guo Moruo

女神之再生

Alles Vergaengliche	一切无常者
ist nur ein Gleichnis;	只是一虚影;
das Unzulaengliche,	不可企及者
hier wird's Ereignis;	在此事已成;
das Unbeschreibliche,	不可名状者
hier ist's getan;	在此已实有;
das Ewigweibliche	永恒之女性
zieht uns hinan.	领导我们走。

| ——*Goethe* | ——歌德 |

序幕:不周山中断处。巉岩壁立,左右两相对峙,俨如巫峡两岸,形成天然门阙。阙后现出一片海水,浩淼无际,与天相接。阙前为平地,其上碧草芊绵,上多坠果。阙之两旁石壁上有无数龛穴。龛中各有裸体女像一尊,手中各持种种乐

Rebirth of the Goddesses

All things transitory
But as symbols are sent;
Earth's insufficiency
Here grows to event;
The Indescribable,
Here it is done;
The Woman-soul leadeth us
Upward and on!

Goethe: Faust

A fissure in the Puchou Mountain: its walls rise abruptly. On either side tower up crags, formidable as the Yangtze Gorges, shaped by nature into the semblance of the gateway to a city. Beyond the crags a vast expanse of sea stretches away to merge with the sky. In front of the crags the level ground is carpeted with luxuriant emerald grass strewn with fallen fruit. Innumerable niches pierce the walls of the sentinel crags and in each niche stands the stat-

器作吹奏式。

山上奇木葱茏，叶如枣，花色金黄，尊如玛瑙，花大如木莲，有硕果形如桃而大。山顶白云暧暧，与天色相含混。

上古时代。共工与颛顼争帝之一日，晦冥。

开幕后沉默数分钟，远远有喧嚷之声起。
女神各置乐器，徐徐自壁龛走下，徐徐向四方瞻望。

女神之一
　自从炼就五色彩石
　曾把天孔补全，
　把黑暗驱逐了一半

ue of a nude goddess bearing in her hands some form of stringed or wind instrument which she seems to be playing.

Strange trees grow profusely on the mountainsides. Their leaves are like those of the date palm; the flowers are golden in colour, with calices like agate. The flowers are large as magnolias; the ripe fruits are shaped like peaches but somewhat larger. Over the summit of the mountain hang massy white clouds, hardly distinguishable against the sky.

The time is of the remote past, a day during the struggles for kingship of Kung-kung and Chuan-hsu. It is dark.

When the curtain rises, all is silent and the silence persists for some moments when distant sounds of clamour make themselves heard.

The goddesses lay aside their instruments and slowly step down from their niches. Slowly they look round them.

FIRST GODDESS:
Since when the five-hued rocks were smelted
to fill the cracks in the heavens
darkness has been half driven away

向那天球外边；

在这优美的世界当中，

吹奏起无声的音乐雍融。

不知道月儿圆了多少回，

照着这生命底音波吹送。

女神之二

可是，我们今天的音调，

为什么总是不能和谐？

怕在这宇宙之中，

有什么浩劫要再！——

听呀！那喧嚷着的声音，

愈见高，愈见逼近！

那是海中的涛声？空中的风声？

可还是——罪恶底交鸣？

女神之三

刚才不是有武夫蛮伯之群

打从这不周山下经过？

说是要去争做什么元首……

哦，闹得真是过火！

beyond the bounds of the celestial sphere.
Within this fair world
strains of silent music have married in harmo-
    ny.
How many moons have waxed and waned,
their light reflected on this wafted life-music?
SECOND GODDESS:
But why can we not bring into accord
the measures we play today?
I fear that in this universe
a catastrophe is likely to come upon us again.
Hark! This harsh clamour
ever louder, ever nearer:
is it from the waves in the sea, from wind in
    space,
or can it be the counterpoint of evil cries?
THIRD GODDESS:
Were they not the barbarous hordes
that passed by the foot of this very Puchou
    Mountain?
They go, they said, to fight for some paltry he-
    gemony;
this turbulence has become intolerable.

姊妹们呀,我们该做什么?

我们这五色天球看看要被震破!

倦了的太阳只在空中睡眠,

全也不吐放些儿炽烈的光波。

女神之一

我要去创造些新的光明,

不能再在这壁龛之中做神。

女神之二

我要去创造些新的温热,

好同你新造的光明相结。

女神之三

姊妹们,新造的葡萄酒浆

不能盛在那旧了的皮囊。

为容受你们的新热、新光,

我要去创造个新鲜的太阳!

其他全体

我们要去创造个新鲜的太阳,

不能再在这壁龛之中做甚神像!

全体向山阙后海中消逝。

8

Sister goddesses, what are we to do?
Our celestial canopy, built of five-coloured
   stone,
may well be shattered in fragments.
The weary sun merely sleeps in space,
no longer shedding its burning waves of light.

FIRST GODDESS:

I will go forth and create new light,
no longer will I remain a mere goddess in a
   niche.

SECOND GODDESS:

I will go forth and create new warmth
to compound with your newly created light.

THIRD GODDESS:

Sister goddesses, new wine may not be con-
tained in old skins.
I will go forth and create a new sun
to contain your new light and new heat.

CHORUS OF GODDESSES:

We will create a new sun,
no longer will we remain mere statues in niches.

The goddesses dissolve into the sea beyond the mountain

山后争帝之声。

颛　项

　　我本是奉天承命的人，

　　上天特命我来统治天下，

　　共工，别教死神来支配你们，

　　快让我做定元首了吧！

共　工

　　我不知道夸说什么上天下地，

　　我是随着我的本心想做皇帝。

　　若有死神时，我便是死神，

　　老颛，你是否还想保存你的老命？

颛　项

　　古人说：天无二日，民无二王。

　　你为什么定要和我对抗？

共　工

　　古人说：民无二王，天无二日。

　　你为什么定要和我争执？

gateway. Behind the mountain rises the clash of embattled
emperors.

CHUAN-HSU:

> I received Heaven's mandate;
>
> Heaven appointed me to rule the world!
>
> Kung-kung, do not let yourselves be caught up
>> by the Spirit of Death;
>
> let me establish my rightful place as leader.

KUNG-KUNG:

> I know nothing about this rant of heaven and
>> earth!
>
> I follow my nature in my desire to be emperor.
>
> If there is to be talk of the Spirit of Death, then
>> I'll deal out death for you.
>
> Chuan-hsu, you had better look out for your
>> own skin!

CHUAN-HSU:

> The ancients had a saying: there cannot be two
>> suns in the sky, nor two rulers among the
>> people.
>
> Why do you press your rivalry to me?

KUNG-KUNG:

> The ancients had a saying: there cannot be two
>> rulers

颛　项

　　啊，你才是个呀——山中的返响！

共　工

　　总之我要满足我的冲动为帝为王！

颛　项

　　你到底为什么定要为帝为王？

共　工

　　你去问那太阳：为什么要亮？

颛　项

　　那么，你只好和我较个短长！

共　工

　　那么，你只好和我较个长短！

群众大呼声

　　战！战！战！

喧呼杀伐声，武器斫击声，血喷声，倒声，步武杂沓声起。

农叟一人（荷耕具穿场而过）

　　我心血都已熬干，

　　麦田中又见有人宣战。

　　黄河之水几时清？

among the people, nor two suns in the sky.

Why are you bent on opposing me?

CHUAN-HSU:

Why, you...you mountain echo!

KUNG-KUNG:

I must satisfy my impulse to become ruler.

CHUAN-HSU:

But what necessity urges you to become ruler?

KUNG-KUNG:

Ask the sun—why must it shine?

CHUAN-HSU:

Then let you try your strength with me.

KUNG-KUNG:

And let you try your strength with me.

Shouts of "War! War! War!" from the massed soldiery.
Clamour of fighting, clashing of weapons, sounds of blood-
spurting, thuds of falling bodies, thunder of trampling feet.

OLD PEASANT (*bearing a ploughshare be makes his way*
across the battlefield):

My heart's blood is quite dried up.

Battle has been joined again over my fields of
corn.

When will the Yellow River run clear,

人的生命几时完?

牧童一人(牵羊群穿场而过)

> 啊,我不该喂了两条斗狗,
>
> 时常只解争吃馒头;
>
> 馒头尽了吃羊头,
>
> 我只好牵着羊儿逃走。

野人之群(执武器从反对方面穿场而过)

> 得寻欢时且寻欢,
>
> 我们要往山后去参战。
>
> 毛头随着风头倒,
>
> 两头利禄好均沾!

山后闻"颛顼万岁! 皇帝万岁!"之声,步武杂沓声,追呼声:"叛逆徒! 你们想往哪儿逃走? 天诛便要到了!"

共　　工(率其党徒自山阙奔出,断发文身,以蕉叶蔽下体,体中随处

when will man's life come to an end?

SHEPHERD BOY (*guiding his flocks across the battle-field*):

> Ah! I should not have reared those fighting
>   dogs,
> usually they fought over crusts of bread,
> but when that was finished they ate heads of
>   sheep.
> I must take my sheep and flee.

A horde of wild men enter. They are armed. They pass across the battlefield from the opposite direction.

WILD MEN:

> Let us make merry while the time favours it.
> Let us go and join the battle beyond the moun-
>   tain.
> The hair bends whither the wind blows:
> Whoever wins we stand to gain.

Beyond the mountain is heard: " Long live Chuan-hsu! Long live the emperor!" Trampling of feet, cries of pursuit: "Traitors, you shall not escape. Heaven is about to strike you down!"

Kung-kung bounds forth from beyond the mountain at the head of his followers. His hair is shorn, his body tattooed, his loins garbed in plantain leaves. There are wounds

受伤,所执铜刀石器亦各鲜血淋漓)

　　啊啊！可恨呀,可恨！

　　可恨我一败涂地！

　　恨不得把那老狯底头颅

　　切来做我饮器！(舐吸武器上血液,作异常愤怒之态)

　　这儿是北方的天柱,不周之山,

　　我的命根已同此山一样中断。

　　党徒们呀！我虽做不成元首,

　　我不肯和那老狯甘休！

　　你们平常仗我为生,

　　我如今要用你们的生命！

　　党徒们拾山下坠果而啖食。

共　　工

　　啊啊,饿瘝之神在我的肚中饥叫！

　　这不周山上的奇果,听说是食之不劳。

　　待到宇宙全体破坏时还有须臾,

on his body; his bronze sword and stone weapons are drip-
ping with fresh blood.

KUNG-KUNG:

Oh shame! Oh, horror! I am utterly defeated.

Would I had the old villain's skull

to carve into a wine-cup!

He licks blood from his weapons and scowls with im-
mense ferocity.

Here is the northern pillar of heaven, the mountain of Puchou;

my life span has been cleft as is this mountain.

Comrades-in-arms, though I may not live to be
king,

I cannot make my peace with that old scoundr-
el.

You have depended on me up to now:

now I have need of your lives.

The followers pick up the fallen fruit and eat of it.

The god of hunger is calling out from our stom-
achs!

They say the magic fruit of Puchou gives unlimited strength to the eater:

there is still a moment before the universe shiv-

你们尽不妨把你们的皮囊装饱。

追呼之声愈迫。

共　工
　　敌人底呼声如像海里的怒涛，
　　只不过逼着这破了的难船早倒！
　　党徒们呀，快把你们的头颅借给我来！
　　快把这北方的天柱碰坏！碰坏！

群以头颅碰山麓岩壁，雷鸣电火四起。少时发一大雷电，山体破裂，天盖倾倒，黑烟一样的物质四处喷涌，共工之徒倒死于山麓。

颛　顼（裸身披发，状如猩猩，率其党徒执同样武器出场）
　　叛逆徒！你们想往那儿逃跑？
　　天诛快……唗呀！唗呀！怎么了？
　　天在飞砂走石，地在震摇，山在爆，

ers asunder.

Go on, get a bellyful of it!

The sound of pursuit becomes more and more insistent.

The war-cries of the foe are like the fury of the
    breakers:

they but hasten this helpless vessel to the bot-
    tom.

My followers! Lend me your skulls!

Crack this northern pillar of heaven!

Crack it!

*The troops rush head foremost against the mountain
wall. Thunder reverberates and lightning plays all round.
Then, a great thunder-clap, the mountain splits apart and
the vault of heaven crashes down. A black cloud billows up.
Kung-kung's followers fall dead at the foot of the mountain.*

CHUAN-HSU (*naked, his hair dishevelled, in build
like a huge ape. He leads his men, armed like himself, from
the battlefield*):

Rebels, where do you think you will flee to?

The gods strike swiftly! Great heavens, what is
    this?

Rocks and stones fly through the air, the earth
    shudders, the mountain is bursting asunder.

啊啊啊啊！浑沌！浑沌！怎么了？怎么了？
　　······

　　雷电愈激愈烈，电火光中照见共工、颛顼及其党徒之尸骸狼籍地上。移时雷电渐渐弛缓，渐就止息。舞台全体尽为黑暗所支配。沉默五分钟。

　　水中游泳之声由远而近。

黑暗中女性之声
　　——雷霆住了声了！
　　——电火已经消灭了！
　　——光明同黑暗底战争已经罢了！
　　——倦了的太阳呢？
　　——被胁迫到天外去了！
　　——天体终竟破了吗？
　　——那被驱逐在天外的黑暗不是都已逃回了吗？
　　——破了的天体怎么处置呀？
　　——再去炼些五色彩石来补好他罢？

Aaaaah. . . ! All is chaos, chaos! What can be
hap-pening?

*The thunder and lightning become more and more
fierce. A flash of lightning reveals the bodies of Kung-kung,
Chuan-hsu and their followers lying scattered about. After a
while the thunderclaps become less violent and gradually die
away. The whole stage is in darkness. Silence of five min-
utes.*

*Sound of swimmers approaching from afar. Women's
voices in the darkness:*

—The thunderclaps have ceased.

—The lightning has died away.

—The battle of light and dark is over.

—What of the weary sun?

—It is driven out of the sky.

—Has the fabric of heaven been torn asunder
after all?

—Have the forces of dark, once driven away,
now crept back?

—What can be done with the rent fabric of
heaven?

—Shall we smelt more coloured stone to repair
it?

——那样五色的东西此后莫中用了！

　　我们尽他破坏不用再补他了！

　　待我们新造的太阳出来，

　　要照彻天内的世界，天外的世界！

　　天球底界限已是莫中用了！

——新造的太阳不怕又要疲倦了吗？

——我们要时常创造新的光明、新的温热去供给

　　她呀！

——哦，我们脚下到处都是男性的残骸呀！

——这又怎么处置呢？

——把他们抬到壁龛之中做起神像来吧！

——不错呀，教他们也奏起无声的音乐来吧！

——新造的太阳，姐姐，怎么还不出来？

——她太热烈了，怕她自行爆裂；

　　还在海水之中浴沐着在！

—Such coloured dross can serve no purpose
now:
however far it is set in decay, we should not
patch it up again.
Let our newly created sun issue forth,
then will it shine through all the inner world
and the outer.
The limits of the celestial sphere serve no
purpose now.
—But the new sun will surely become weary?
—We must be for ever creating new light and
heat for it.
—Ugh! Everywhere underfoot are the remains
of men's bodies.
—What shall we do with them?
—Bear them to the niches and mould them into
gods.
—Yes and set them playing silent music as we
once did.
—The new sun, my sister, why has it not yet
risen?
—It burns too fiercely, we fear it will explode;
we have it still plunged in the sea.

———哦,我们感受着新鲜的暖意了!

———我们的心脏,好像些鲜红的金鱼,

在水晶瓶里跳跃!

———我们什么都想拥抱呀!

———我们唱起歌来欢迎新造的太阳吧!

合唱:

太阳虽还在远方,

太阳虽还在远方,

海水中早听着晨钟在响:

丁当,丁当,丁当。

万千金箭射天狼,

天狼已在暗悲哀,

海水中早听着葬钟在响:

丁当,丁当,丁当。

—Ah! We now feel new warmth.

—Our hearts are like crimson carp,

leaping in a crystal bowl.

—We desire to embrace all things.

—Let us sing a song of welcome to the newly
created sun.

In Unison:

Sun, although you are still far away,

sun, although you are still far away,

now the morning bell can be heard pealing in
the sea:

ding-dong, ding-dong, ding-dong!

Ten thousand golden arrows shoot at the Wolf
of Heaven;

the Wolf of Heaven grieves in the dark.

Now the funeral knell can be heard in the sea:

ding-dong, ding-dong, ding-dong!

We wish to quaff a stoup of wine.

Drink to the everlasting life of our new sun.

Now the drinking bells sound in the sea:

ding-dong, ding-dong, ding-dong!

我们欲饮葡萄觥，
愿祝新阳寿无疆，
海水中早听着酒钟在响：
丁当，丁当，丁当。

此时舞台突然光明，只现一张白幕。舞台监督登场。

舞台监督(向听众一鞠躬)诸君！你们在乌烟瘴气的黑暗世
界当中怕已经坐倦了吧！怕在渴慕着光明了
吧！作这幕诗剧的诗人做到这儿便停了笔，他
真正逃往海外去造新的光明和新的热力去了。
诸君，你们要望新生的太阳出现吗？还是请去
自行创造来！我们待太阳出现时再会！

〔附白〕此剧取材于下引各文中：

天地亦物也，物有不足，故昔者女娲氏炼五色石以补其
缺，断鳌之足以立四极。其后共工氏与颛顼争为帝，怒而触

26

The stage suddenly lights up. Only a white curtain is to be seen.

The stage-manager appears.

STAGE-MANAGER (*bows to the audience*):

Ladies and gentlemen, you have become tired of living in the foetid gloom of this dark world. You surely thirst for light. Your poet, having dramatized so far, writes no more. He has, in fact, fled beyond the sea to create new light and heat. Ladies and gentlemen, do you await the appearance of a new sun? You are bid to create it for yourselves. We will meet again under the new sun.

Notes

Material for the play has been taken from the following sources:

Lieh Tzu (ancient Taoist philosophical work): "...Heaven and earth are also material things, and things are subject to deficiencies. Hence in ancient times the goddess Nu-kua forged five-coloured rocks to fill in the cracks, and broke off the turtle's feet and set them up as the four pillars of the sky. Thereafter, when Kungkung struggled with Chuan-hsu for

不周之山。折天柱,绝地维。故天倾西北,日月星辰就焉;地不满东南,故百川水潦归焉。(《列子》:《汤问篇》)

女娲氏古之神圣女,化万物者也。——始制笙簧。(《说文》)

不周之山北望诸毗之山,临彼岳崇之山,东望泑泽(别名蒲昌海),河水所潜也;其源浑浑泡泡。爰有嘉果,其实如桃,其叶如枣,黄华而赤柎,食之不劳。(《山海经》:《西次三经》)

kingship, in his fury he threw himself against Puchou Mountain. He snapped this pillar of heaven and upset the balance of the four-cornered earth. As a result, the sky tilted down at the northwest corner, so that the sun, the moon and the stars now move in that direction. The earth being inclined in the southeast, all watercourses drain away thither."

Shuo Wen (the Han dynasty dictionary): "Nu-kua was an ancient goddess, who shaped the ten thousand things....

She first invented the pipes and flute."

Shan Hai Ching (ancient book of folklore and legends):

"To the north, the Puchou Mountain faces Chu-pi Mountain, and Yuehchung Mountain is not far away; to the east it faces the salt marsh of Yu, which is where the Yellow River disappears underground after leaving its turbid, seething source. Here there are delicious fruits which are like peaches; the leaves are like those of the jujube tree and the flowers are yellow with a red calyx. These fruits can refresh one when one is fatigued."

凤凰涅槃

天方国古有神鸟名"菲尼克司"（*Phoenix*），满五百岁后，集香木自焚，复从死灰中更生，鲜美异常，不再死。

按此鸟殆即中国所谓凤凰：雄为凤，雌为凰。《孔演图》云："凤凰火精，生丹穴。"《广雅》云："凤凰……雄鸣曰即即，雌鸣曰足足。"

序　　曲

除夕将近的空中，
飞来飞去的一对凤凰，
唱着哀哀的歌声飞去，
衔着枝枝的香木飞来，

The Nirvana of the
Feng and Huang

In Arabia in ancient times there lived a magical bird, the phoenix. When it had reached the age of 500 years, it made a pyre of fragrant wood and committed itself to the flames. Then from the dead ashes it returned to life never to die again with a fresh and extraordinary beauty.

Now, this bird may well be the Feng-Huang bird of China. The Feng is the male, the Huang the female. In the Yen Kung Tu (Elucidation of the Illustrations of Confucius) we read: "The Feng-Huang is the essence of fire; it is born on Mount Tanhsueh." According to the Kuang Ya dictionary: "As to the Feng-Huang... the cry of the male bird is jig-jig, that of the female bird is jug-jug."

Prelude

The eve of the new year is at hand and in the
  sky
the Feng-Huang pair dart here and about.
Mournful strains are heard as they fly away,
bearing fragrant twigs in their bills they return,

飞来在丹穴山上。

山右有枯槁了的梧桐，
山左有消歇了的醴泉，
山前有浩茫茫的大海，
山后有阴莽莽的平原，
山上是寒风凛冽的冰天。

天色昏黄了，
香木集高了，
凤已飞倦了，
凰已飞倦了，
他们的死期将近了。

凤啄香木，
一星星的火点迸飞。
凰扇火星，
一缕缕的香烟上腾。

凤又啄，

fly back to the Tanhsueh Mountain.

To the right is the withered plane tree,
to the left the parched spring;
before the mountain the limitless expanse of the
   sea,
behind it the vast dismal plains,
over the mountain the frozen sky traversed by
   icy winds.

The sky is now dark with evening,
the fragrant wood is heaped high.
The Feng is weary with flying,
the Huang is weary with flying;
their hour of death approaches.

The Feng pecks the twigs:
points of flame fly out.
The Huang fans the sparks:
wreaths of fragrant smoke rise up.

The Feng pecks on

凰又扇，
山上的香烟弥散，
山上的火光弥满。

夜色已深了，
香木已燃了，
凤已啄倦了，
凰已扇倦了，
他们的死期已近了！

啊啊！
哀哀的凤凰！
凤起舞，低昂！
凰唱歌，悲壮！
凤又舞，
凰又唱，
一群的凡鸟，
自天外飞来观葬。

凤　歌

即即！即即！即即！
即即！即即！即即！
茫茫的宇宙，冷酷如铁！

and the Huang fans the flame.
The fragrant smoke overspreads the peak,
the glow of the fire suffuses the peak.

The dusk has now deepened,
the fragrant wood is burning.
The Feng is weary with pecking,
the Huang is weary with fanning:
their hour of death is at hand.

Alas for the Feng and Huang!
The Feng dances, dances high and low,
the Huang sings, sings in tragic vein.
The Feng dances,
the Huang sings her song.
The commonalty of birds flock thither,
fly in from the skies to witness the death-rite.

Song of the Feng

Jig-jig, jig-jig, jig-jig,
Jig-jig, jig-jig, jig-jig.
Vast is the universe, cruel as iron.

茫茫的宇宙,黑暗如漆!
茫茫的宇宙,腥秽如血!

宇宙呀,宇宙,
你为什么存在?
你自从哪儿来?
你坐在哪儿在?
你是个有限大的空球?
你是个无限大的整块?
你若是有限大的空球,
那拥抱着你的空间
他从哪儿来?
你的外边还有些什么存在?
你若是无限大的整块,
这被你拥抱着的空间
他从哪儿来?
你的当中为什么又有生命存在?
你到底还是个有生命的交流?
你到底还是个无生命的机械?

昂头我问天,
天徒矜高,莫有点儿知识。

Vast is the universe, sombre as lacquer.
Vast is the universe, rank as blood.

Universe, O universe!
Why do you exist?
Whence do you come?
Where are you cradled?
Are you an empty sphere limited in reach,
or a continuum of unlimited size?
If you are an empty sphere limited in reach
whence comes the space that contains you?
What else has existence outside yourself?
If you are infinite and all-embracing
whence comes the space that you hold in your-
    self?
And why does life exist within you?
Are you a life-endowed flux,
or are you a lifeless mechanism?

I raise my brow and ask of Heaven,
but Heaven is reserved and aloof, has no knowl-
    edge of these things.

低头我问地，
地已死了，莫有点儿呼吸。
伸头我问海，
海正扬声而鸣唈。

啊啊！
生在这样个阴秽的世界当中，
便是把金钢石的宝刀也会生锈！
宇宙呀，宇宙，
我要努力地把你诅咒：
你脓血污秽着的屠场呀！
你悲哀充塞着的囚牢呀！
你群鬼叫号着的坟墓呀！
你群魔跳梁着的地狱呀！
你到底为什么存在？
我们飞向西方，
西方同是一座屠场。
我们飞向东方，
东方同是一座囚牢。
我们飞向南方，
南方同是一座坟墓。

I bend my brow and ask the earth,
but the earth is dead, it has no breath.
I look out and ask the sea,
but the sea is raising its voice in grieving.

Ah!
To exist in the mire and gloom of this world
would cause even a diamond sword to rust.
Universe, O universe,
let me rail at you with all my powers:
you blood-besmirched slaughter-house,
prison surfeited with misery,
graveyard clamorous with ghostly hordes,
hell astir with capering demons,
why should you exist at all?

We fly westwards:
the west, alike, is a slaughter-house.
We fly eastwards:
the east, alike, is a prison.
We fly southwards:
the south, alike, is a grave.

我们飞向北方，
北方同是一座地狱。
我们生在这样个世界当中，
只好学着海洋哀哭。

凰　歌

足足！足足！足足！
足足！足足！足足！
五百年来的眼泪倾泻如瀑。
五百年来的眼泪淋漓如烛。
流不尽的眼泪，
洗不净的污浊，
浇不熄的情炎，
荡不去的羞辱，
我们这缥缈的浮生
到底要向哪儿安宿？

啊啊！
我们这缥缈的浮生
好像那大海里的孤舟。
左也是漂漫，

We fly northwards:
the north, alike, is a hell.
Living in such a world
we can but learn from the lament of the sea.

Song of the Huang

Jug-jug, jug-jug, jug-jug,
Jug-jug, jug-jug, jug-jug.
Five hundred years of tears have streamed like
    a cataract,
five hundred years of tears have dripped like
    wax from candle.
Unceasing flow of tears,
filth that cannot be washed away,
flame of passion that cannot be extinguished,
shame that cannot be cleansed.
This shadowy life of ours,
towards what haven is it drifting?

Ah, this dreamy, shadowy life of ours
is like a lonely boat on an ocean:
to the right are trackless waters,

右也是滉漾，
前不见灯台，
后不见海岸，
帆已破，
樯已断，
楫已飘流，
柁已腐烂，
倦了的舟子只是在舟中呻唤，
怒了的海涛还是在海中泛滥。

啊啊！
我们这缥缈的浮生
好像这黑夜里的酣梦。
前也是睡眠，
后也是睡眠，
来得如飘风，
去得如轻烟，
来如风，
去如烟，
眠在后，
睡在前，
我们只是这睡眠当中的

to the left are trackless waters.
No beacon shines ahead,
no shore is seen behind.
The sail is torn,
the mast broken,
the oars have floated away,
the rudder has rotted away.
The weary boatman merely sits and moans,
the angry surge rolls over in the sea.

Ah, this shadowy, drifting life of ours
is like a drugged sleep on such a dark night as
   this.
Before us is sleep,
behind us is sleep.
We come like a gust of wind,
we go like a whisp of smoke.
Coming like wind,
going like smoke,
sleep behind,
sleep before.
In the midst of this sleep

一刹那的风烟。

啊啊！
有什么意思？
有什么意思？
痴！痴！痴！
只剩些悲哀，烦恼，寂寥，衰败，
环绕着我们活动着的死尸，
贯串着我们活动着的死尸。

啊啊！
我们年青时候的新鲜哪儿去了？
我们年青时候的甘美哪儿去了？
我们年青时候的光华哪儿去了？
我们年青时候的欢爱哪儿去了？
去了！去了！去了！
一切都已去了，
一切都要去了。
我们也要去了，
你们也要去了，

we are but a fleeting breath of smoke.

Ah!
What sense is there in it?
What sense is there in it?
Folly...folly...folly!
There remains only grief, vexation, desolation,
   decay,
a back-cloth for our living corpses,
a thread running through the lives of our living
   corpses.

Ah!
Where is now the freshness of our youth?
Where is now the sweetness of our youth?
Where is now the splendour of our youth?
Where is now the pleasure of our youth?
Gone! Gone! Gone!
All is gone!
All must go!
We are gone.
You too must go.

悲哀呀！烦恼呀！寂寥呀！衰败呀！

凤凰同歌

啊啊！
火光熊熊了。
香气蓬蓬了。
时期已到了。
死期已到了。
身外的一切！
身内的一切！
一切的一切！
请了！请了！

群鸟歌

岩　鹰
　　哈哈，凤凰！凤凰！
　　你们枉为这禽中的灵长！
　　你们死了吗？你们死了吗？
　　从今后该我为空界的霸王！
孔　雀
　　哈哈，凤凰！凤凰！

46

Grief...vexation...desolation...decay.

Ah!
The fire flares dazzling bright,
the fragrant smoke hangs heavily in the air.
My time has now come,
my hour of death has come,
all within us,
all outside us,
all in all.
Farewell! Farewell!

Choral song of the birds

EAGLE:

Haha! Feng-Huang! Feng-Huang!
In vain have you been the most magical of
birds.
Are you dead? Are you dead?
Henceforth must I assert my sway over the aeri-
al world.

PEACOCK:

Haha! Feng-Huang! Feng-Huang!

你们枉为这禽中的灵长！
你们死了吗？你们死了吗？
从今后请看我花翎上的威光！

鸱　枭

哈哈，凤凰！凤凰！
你们枉为这禽中的灵长！
你们死了吗？你们死了吗？
哦！是哪儿来的鼠肉的馨香？

家　鸽

哈哈，凤凰！凤凰！
你们枉为这禽中的灵长！
你们死了吗？你们死了吗？
从今后请看我们驯良百姓的安康！

鹦　鹉

哈哈，凤凰！凤凰！
你们枉为这禽中的灵长！

In vain have you been the most magical of
   birds.
Are you dead? Are you dead?
Henceforth let you behold the royal sheen of my
   plumage.

OWL:

Haha! Feng-Huang! Feng-Huang!
In vain have you been the most magical of
   birds.
Are you dead? Are you dead?
Whence comes this sweet fragrance of mouse
   flesh?

PIGEON:

Haha! Feng-Huang! Feng-Huang!
In vain have you been the most magical of
   birds.
Are you dead? Are you dead?
Henceforth you may see the contentment of our
   docile tribe

PAEEOT:

Haha! Feng-Huang! Feng-Huang!
In vain have you been the most magical of

你们死了吗？你们死了吗？
从今后请听我们雄辩家的主张！

白　鹤

哈哈，凤凰！凤凰！
你们枉为这禽中的灵长！
你们死了吗？你们死了吗？
从今后请看我们高蹈派的徜徉！

凤凰更生歌

鸡　鸣

昕潮涨了，
昕潮涨了，
死了的光明更生了。

春潮涨了，
春潮涨了，
死了的宇宙更生了。

50

birds.

Are you dead? Are you dead?

Henceforth listen to the eloquent discourses of
our orators.

STORK:

Haha! Feng-Huang! Feng-Huang!

In vain have you been the most magical of
birds.

Are you dead? Are you dead?

Henceforth see the strutting to and fro of our
high-stepping race.

Rebirth song of the Feng and Huang

COCKS:

The tide of dawn has risen,
the tide of dawn has risen,
the light that died is born anew.

The tide of spring has risen,
the tide of spring has risen,
the cosmos that died is born anew.

生潮涨了，
生潮涨了，
死了的凤凰更生了。
凤凰和鸣

我们更生了。
我们更生了。
一切的一，更生了。
一的一切，更生了。
我们便是他，他们便是我。
我中也有你，你中也有我。
我便是你。
你便是我。
火便是凰。
凤便是火。
翱翔！翱翔！
欢唱！欢唱！

我们新鲜，我们净朗，
我们华美，我们芬芳，
一切的一，芬芳。
一的一切，芬芳。
芬芳便是你，芬芳便是我。
芬芳便是他，芬芳便是火。

The tide of life has risen,

the tide of life has risen,

the Feng and Huang that died are born anew.

FENG AND HUANG SING TOGETHER:

We are born again,

we are born again.

The one that is all is born again,

the all that is one is born again.

We are he, they are me,

you are in me and I in you:

I am therefore you,

you are therefore me.

The fire is the Huang,

the Feng is the fire.

Soar then, soar!

Sing for joy, sing for joy!

We are made anew, we are purified.

We are resplendent, we are steeped in fragrance.

The one that is all is steeped in fragrance,

the all that is one is steeped in fragrance.

Fragrance steeped are you, fragrance steeped am I,

fragrance steeped is he, fragrance steedped is fire.

火便是你。
火便是我。
火便是他。
火便是火。
翱翔！翱翔！
欢唱！欢唱！

我们热诚，我们挚爱。
我们欢乐，我们和谐。
一切的一，和谐。
一的一切，和谐。
和谐便是你，和谐便是我。
和谐便是他，和谐便是火。
火便是你。
火便是我。
火便是他。
火便是火。
翱翔！翱翔！
欢唱！欢唱！

我们生动，我们自由，
我们雄浑，我们悠久。
一切的一，悠久。
一的一切，悠久。

Fire are you,
fire am I,
fire is he,
fire is fire.
Soar then, soar!
Sing for joy, sing for joy!
We are pledged, we are deeply in love,
we are devoted, we are truly matched.
The one that is all is truly matched,
the all that is one is truly matched.
Truly matched are you, truly matched am I,
truly matched is he, truly matched is fire.
Fire are you,
fire am I,
fire is he,
fire is fire.
Soar then, soar!
Sing for joy, sing for joy!
We are vigorous, we are free,
we are fearless, we are immortal.
The one that is all is immortal,
the all that is one is immortal.

悠久便是你,悠久便是我。
悠久便是他,悠久便是火。
火便是你。
火便是我。
火便是他。
火便是火。
翱翔!翱翔!
欢唱!欢唱!

我们欢唱,我们翱翔。
我们翱翔,我们欢唱。
一切的一,常在欢唱。
一的一切,常在欢唱。
是你在欢唱?是我在欢唱?
是他在欢唱?是火在欢唱?
欢唱在欢唱!
欢唱在欢唱!
只有欢唱!
只有欢唱!
欢唱!
　欢唱!
　　欢唱!

1920 年 1 月 20 日初稿
1928 年 1 月 3 日改削

56

Immortal are you, immortal am I,
Immortal is he, immortal is fire.
    Fire am I,
    fire are you,
    fire is he,
    fire is fire.
    Soar then, soar!
Sing for joy, sing for joy!
We sing for joy, we soar,
we soar, we sing for joy!
The one that is all sings for joy,
the all that is one sings for joy.
    Is it you who sing for joy, or is it I?
    Is it he who sings for joy, or is it fire?
    It is joy itself that sings for joy!
    It is joy itself that sings for joy!
    Only joyfully singing,
    only joyfully singing!
Singing!
    Singing!
    Singing!

Draft: January 20, 1920
Revised: January 3, 1928

炉中煤

——眷念祖国的情绪

啊，我年青的女郎！
我不辜负你的殷勤，
你也不要辜负了我的思量。
我为我心爱的人儿
燃到了这般模样！

啊，我年青的女郎！
你该知道了我的前身？
你该不嫌我黑奴卤莽？
要我这黑奴的胸中，
才有火一样的心肠。

啊，我年青的女郎！
我想我的前身
原本是有用的栋梁，
我活埋在地底多年，
到今朝总得重见天光。

Coal in the Grate

– Dedicated to my native land

Ah, my fair young maiden,
I shall not betray your care,
let you not disappoint my hopes.
For her my heart's delight
I burn to such a heat.

Ah, my fair young maiden,
you must know of my former life.
You cannot shrink from my coarseness:
only in such a breast as mine
could burn a fire so bright.

Ah, my fair young maiden,
certain it is that in my former life
I was a trusty pillar
buried alive for years on end:
today must I see the light of day again.

啊，我年青的女郎！
我自从重见天光，
我常常思念我的故乡，
我为我心爱的人儿
燃到了这般模样！

1920 年 1、2 月间作

Ah, my fair young maiden,
since I see the light of day again
I think only of my native home:
for her my heart's delight
I burn to such a heat.

January – February 1920

日　出

哦哦,环天都是火云!
好像是赤的游龙,赤的狮子,
赤的鲸鱼,赤的象,赤的犀。
你们可都是亚坡罗的前驱?

哦哦,摩托车前的明灯!
你二十世纪底亚坡罗!
你也改乘了摩托车吗?
我想做个你的助手,你肯同意吗?

哦哦,光的雄劲!
玛瑙一样的晨鸟在我眼前飞腾。
明与暗,刀切断了一样地分明!
这正是生命和死亡的斗争!

哦哦,明与暗,同是一样的浮云。

Sunrise

Fiery clouds girdle the rim of the sky
like crimson dragons roving the air,
like crimson lions, whales, elephants, rhinocer-
    oses.
Perhaps you are all outriders of Apollo?

And you, blazling headlights of motorcars,
you twentieth-century Apollos,
have you not changed your mount for a car?
I would be your driver, will you engage me?

Ah! The vitality of light!
Agate morning birds scatter before my eyes.
Light and dark are divided with the clean cut of
    a knife.
For light there are floating clouds, for dark
    there are floating clouds.

我守看着那一切的暗云……
被亚坡罗的雄光驱除干净！
是凯旋的鼓吹呵，四野的鸡声！

1920 年 3 月间作

Both are floating clouds, why then dark, why
   light?
I hold my gaze on the darkness of the clouds:
all are dispersed by Apollo's potent beams.
Then I saw that the cockcrows all about me
   have a deeper meaning.

                                    March 1920

晨 安

晨安！常动不息的大海呀！
晨安！明迷恍惚的旭光呀！
晨安！诗一样涌着的白云呀！
晨安！平匀明直的丝雨呀！诗语呀！
晨安！情热一样燃着的海山呀！
晨安！梳人灵魂的晨风呀！
晨风呀！你请把我的声音传到四方去吧！

晨安！我年青的祖国呀！
晨安！我新生的同胞呀！
晨安！我浩荡荡的南方的扬子江呀！

The Good Morning

I greet you with a Good Morning,
rolling ocean that knows no rest,
shimmering glow of the rosy dawn,
white clouds welling up like poetry from its
    source.
silken rain-threads evenly drawn(language of
    poetry),
crests over the sea burning with the fire of pas-
    sion,
morning breeze combing the soul.
(Morning breeze, bear away my voice to the
    four quarters!)

I greet you with a Good Morning,
my youthful homeland,
my new-born kinsfolk,
boundless reaches in southern lands of my Yan-
    gtze,

晨安！我冻结着的北方的黄河呀！
黄河呀！我望你胸中的冰块早早融化呀！
晨安！万里长城呀！
啊啊！雪的旷野呀！
啊啊！我所畏敬的俄罗斯呀！
晨安！我所畏敬的 *Pioneer* 呀！
晨安！雪的帕米尔呀！
晨安！雪的喜玛拉雅呀！
晨安！*Bengal* 的泰戈尔翁呀！
晨安！自然学园里的学友们呀！
晨安！恒河呀！恒河里面流泻着的灵光呀！
晨安！印度洋呀！红海呀！苏彝士的运河呀！
晨安！尼罗河畔的金字塔呀！
啊啊！你早就幻想飞行的达·芬奇！
晨安！你坐在万神祠前面的"沉思者"呀！
晨安！半工半读团的学友们呀！
晨安！比利时呀！比利时的遗民呀！
晨安！爱尔兰呀！爱尔兰的诗人呀！
啊啊！大西洋呀！

frozen wastes in northern lands of my Yellow
  River.
(Yellow River, may the ice-floes in your bosom
  thaw very soon!)
Thousand-league Great Wall,
wilderness of snow,
the Russia who inspires me with awe,
the pioneer I hold in awe.

I greet you with a Good Morning,
snow-capped Pamirs,
snow-capped Himalayas,
revered Tagore of Bengal,
fellow scholars in the school of Nature,
Ganges! Sacred light glowing on the Ganges,
Indian Ocean, Red Sea, Suez Canal,
pyramids on the banks of the Nile!
Da Vinci, so early your dreams of flight,
Thinkerof Rodin, seated before the Pantheon,
band of friends, half working half studying,
Belgium, people of Belgium, survivors of war,
Ireland, poets of Ireland,
Atlantic!

晨安！大西洋呀！

晨安！大西洋畔的新大陆呀！

晨安！华盛顿的墓呀！林肯的墓呀！惠特曼
　　的墓呀！

啊啊！惠特曼呀！惠特曼呀！太平洋一样的
　　惠特曼呀！

啊啊！太平洋呀！

晨安！太平洋呀！太平洋上的诸岛呀！太平
　　洋上的扶桑呀！

扶桑呀！扶桑呀！还在梦里裹着的扶桑呀！

醒呀！*Mésamé* 呀！

快来享受这千载一时的晨光呀！

1920 年 1 月间作

I greet you with a Good Morning,
Atlantic, flanked by the New World,
grave of Washington, of Lincoln, of Whitman,
Whitman! Whitman! The Pacific that was
   Whitman!
Pacific!
Pacific Ocean! Isles of the Pacific, ancient Fu-
   sang lying in the Pacific,
O Fusang! Fusang still wrapped in dream.
Awake! *Mésamé*!
Hasten to share in this millennial dawn!

                              January 1920

笔立山头展望

大都会的脉搏呀！
生的鼓动呀！
打着在,吹着在,叫着在,……
喷着在,飞着在,跳着在,……
四面的天郊烟幕蒙笼了！
我的心脏呀,快要跳出口来了！
哦哦,山岳的波涛,瓦屋的波涛,
涌着在,涌着在,涌着在,涌着在呀！
万籁共鸣的 *symphony*,
自然与人生的婚礼呀！
弯弯的海岸好像 *Cupid* 的弓弩呀！
人的生命便是箭,正在海上放射呀！
黑沈沈的海湾,停泊着的轮船,进行着的轮船,
　数不尽的轮船,
一枝枝的烟筒都开着了朵黑色的牡丹呀！
哦哦,二十世纪的名花！
近代文明的严母呀！

1920 年 6 月间作

Panorama from Fudetate Yama

Pulse of the great city,
surge of life,
beating, panting, roaring,
spurting, flying, leaping,
the whole sky covered with a pall of smoke;
my heart is ready to leap from my mouth.
Hills, roofs, surge on,
wave after wave they well up before me.
Symphony of myriad sounds,
marriage of man and Nature.
The curve of the bay might be Cupid's bow,
man's life his arrow, shot over the sea.
Dark and misty coastline, steamers at anchor,
steamers in motion, steamers unnumbered,
funnel upon funnel bearing its black peony.
Ah! Emblem of the Twentieth Century!
Stern mother of modern civilization!

June 1920

立在地球边上放号

无数的白云正在空中怒涌,

啊啊!好幅壮丽的北冰洋的晴景哟!

无限的太平洋提起他全身的力量来要把地球推
　倒。

啊啊!我眼前来了的滚滚的洪涛哟!

啊啊!不断的毁坏,不断的创造,不断的努力
　哟!

啊啊!力哟!力哟!

力的绘画,力的舞蹈,力的音乐,力的诗歌,力的
　律吕哟!

1919 年 9、10 月间作

Shouting on the
Rim of the World

Endless tumult of angry white clouds,
sublime arctic landscape.
The mighty Pacific gathers her strength to en-
   gulf the earth,
the surging flood wells up before me:
unending destruction, unending creation, unending effort.
Ah, power, power!
Picture of power, dance of power, music of
   power, poetry of
   power, gamut of power!

September – October 1919

三个泛神论者

一

我爱我国的庄子，
因为我爱他的 *Pantheism*，
因为我爱他是靠打草鞋吃饭的人。

二

我爱荷兰的 *Spinoza*，
因为我爱他的 *Pantheism*，
因为我爱他是靠磨镜片吃饭的人。

三

我爱印度的 *Kabir*，
因为我爱他的 *Pantheism*，
因为我爱他是靠编鱼网吃饭的人。

Three Pantheists

I love our old Chuang-tzu
because I love his pantheism,
because he got a living by making straw shoes.

I love the Dutchman Spinoza
because I love his pantheism,
because he got a living by grinding lenses.

I love the Indian Kabir
because I love his pantheism,
because he got a living by knotting fishing-nets.

电火光中

一 怀古——贝加尔湖畔之苏子卿

电灯已着了光，
我的心儿却怎这么幽暗？
我孤独地在市中徐行，
想到了苏子卿在贝加尔湖湖畔。
我想象他披着一件白羊裘，
毡履，毡裳，毡巾复首，
独立在苍茫无际的西比利亚荒原当中，
有雪潮一样的羊群在他背后。
我想象他在个孟春的黄昏时分，待要归返穹庐，
背景中贝加尔湖上的冰涛，
与天际的白云波连山竖。

By Electric Light

I. *Inspired by an old theme:*
Su Tse-ching by Lake Baikal

The electric lights are already shining,
but why is there gloom in my heart?
I pace, a lone figure, in the city;
I think of Su Tse-ching on the shores of Lake
   Baikal.
I see him with his white fleece on his shoulde-
   rs,
a felt turban on his head, felt shoes, felt gown,
a solitary figure in the boundless Siberian
   steppes,
behind him a snowy sea of sheep.
I see him at dusk in early spring,
waiting to return to the yurt,
his background the frozen waves of Lake Baikal
whose shapes mingle with the undulations of

我想象他向着东行，
遥遥地正望南翘首；
眼眸中含蓄着无限的悲哀，
又好像燃着希望一缕。

二 观画——Millet 的"牧羊少女"

电灯已着了光，
我的心儿却怎这么幽暗？
我想象着苏子卿的乡思，
我步进了街头的一家画馆。
我赏玩了一回四林湖畔的日晡，
我又在加里弗尼亚州观望瀑布——
哦，好一幅理想的画图！理想以上的画图！
画中的人！你可不便是胡妇吗？胡妇！
一个野花烂缦的碧绿的大平原，

the clouds at the horizon.
I see him moving eastwards,
far away, looking towards the south, his head
   raised,
his eyes charged with infinite sorrow,
and yet as though there burned a thread of
   hope.

II . *Before a painting,*
the Shepherdess of Millet

The electric lights are already shining,
but why is there gloom in my heart?
I imagine Su Tse-ching's thoughts turning to
   home.
I enter an art gallery from the street,
I enjoy the late afternoon scene of
   Vierwaldstätter Sea;
next I gaze on a waterfall in California—
an ideal picture, a picture more than ideal.
Person in the painting, surely you are a barbari-
   an woman, yes a barbarian woman.
A vast emerald plain brilliant with wild flowers

在我的面前展放。
平原中立着一个持杖的女人，
背后也涌着了一群归羊。
那怕是苏武归国后的风光，
他的弃妻，他的群羊无恙；
可那牧羊女人的眼中，眼中，
那含蓄的悲愤？怨望？凄凉？

三　赞像——Beethoven 的肖像

电灯已着了光，
我的心儿却怎这么幽暗？
我望着那弥勒的画图，
我又在"世界名画集"中寻检。
圣母，耶稣的头，抱破瓶的少女……
在我面前翩舞。
哦，贝多芬！贝多芬！
你解除了我无名的愁苦！

unrolls before my eyes.

In it stands a woman with a crook in her hand,

at her back, homeward-bound, surges her flock
of sheep.

Such must have been the scene from which Su
Tse-ching returned:

his forsaken wife, his thriving flock.

But the eyes of the shepherdess, those eyes...

are they fraught with bitterness, with resent-
ment or with despair?

Ⅲ. *Portrait of Beethoven*

The electric lights are already shining,

but why is there gloom in my heart?

I look at the painting by Millet,

I again search throughThe World's Great Paint-
ers.

The Mother, head of Jesus, girl hugging a pitch-
er...

dance before my eyes.

Ah! Beethoven! Beethoven! You dispel my
nameless grief!

你蓬蓬的乱发如像奔流的海涛，
你高张的白领如像戴雪的山椒。
你如狮的额，如虎的眼，
你这如像"大宇宙意志"自身的头脑！
你右手持着铅笔，左手持着原稿，
你那笔尖头上正在倾泻着怒潮。
贝多芬哟！你可在倾听什么？
我好像听着你的 *symphony* 了！

1919 年年末初稿
1928 年 2 月 1 日修改

Your dishevelled hair streams like swiftly flowing waves,
your high white collar is like a snow-capped
ridge;
your leonine forehead, your tigerish eyes,
your brain which is like"the will of the Universe"itself.
In your right hand a pen, in your left a manu-
script,
an angry torrent flows from the point of your
pen.
Beethoven! What are you listening to?
It is as if I were hearing your Symphony.

Draft: end of 1919
Revised: February I, 1928

地球,我的母亲!

地球,我的母亲!
天已黎明了,
你把你怀中的儿来摇醒,
我现在正在你背上匍行。

地球,我的母亲!
你背负着我在这乐园中逍遥。
你还在那海洋里面,
奏出些音乐来,安慰我的灵魂。

地球,我的母亲!
我过去,现在,未来,
食的是你,衣的是你,住的是你,
我要怎么样才能够报答你的深恩?

地球,我的母亲!

O Earth, My Mother

O earth, my mother,
the sky is already pale with dawn;
you rouse the child in your bosom,
now I am crawling on your back.

O earth, my mother,
you sustain me as I roam through the paradisia-
   cal garden,
and within the ocean
you give forth music that soothes my spirit.

O earth, my mother,
through past, present, future
you are food, apparel, shelter for me;
how can I repay the benefits you have bestowed
   upon me?

O earth, my mother,

从今后我不愿常在家中居住，
我要常在这开旷的空气里面，
对于你，表示我的孝心。

地球，我的母亲！
我羡慕你的孝子，田地里的农人，
他们是全人类的保母，
你是时常地爱抚他们。

地球，我的母亲！
我羡慕你的宠子，炭坑里的工人，
他们是全人类的普罗美修士，
你是时常地怀抱着他们。

地球，我的母亲！
我羡慕那一切的草木，我的同胞，你的儿孙，
他们自由地，自主地，随分地，健康地，
享受着他们的赋生。

henceforth I shall seclude myself less indoors;
in the midst of this opening up of waste lands
I would fulfil my filial duty to you.

O earth, my mother,
I am envious of your dutiful sons, the peasants
   in the fields;
they are the nurse of mankind,
you have always cared for them.

O earth, my mother,
I am envious of your darlings, workers in coal-
   pits;
they are the Prometheus of mankind,
you have always cared for them.

O earth, my mother,
I am envious of every blade or twig, my broth-
   ers, your progeny:
freely, independently, contentedly, vigorously
they enjoy the life bestowed on them.

地球，我的母亲！
我羡慕那一切的动物，尤其是蚯蚓——
我只不羡慕那空中的飞鸟：
他们离了你要在空中飞行。
地球，我的母亲！
我不愿在空中飞行，
我也不愿坐车，乘马，著袜，穿鞋，
我只愿赤裸着我的双脚，永远和你相亲。

地球，我的母亲！
你是我实有性的证人，
我不相信你只是个梦幻泡影，
我不相信我只是个妄执无明。

地球，我的母亲！
我们都是空桑中生出的伊尹，
我不相信那缥缈的天上，

O earth, my mother,
I envy every living creature, the earthworm
    most of all;
only I do not envy the birds flying in the air,
they have left you to go their way in the air.

O earth, my mother,
I do not wish to fly in the air,
nor ride in carts, on horseback, wear socks or
    put on shoes,
I only wish to go barefoot, ever closer to you.

O earth, my mother,
you are witness to the reality of my existence;
I do not believe you are the mere shape of a
    bubble conjured forth in a dream,
I do not believe I am merely an imbecile crea-
    ture acting without reason.

O earth, my mother,
we are all I-yin, born out of Kungsang;
I do not believe that in the shadowy heaven

还有位什么父亲。

地球，我的母亲！
我想这宇宙中的一切都是你的化身：
雷霆是你呼吸的声威，
雪雨是你血液的飞腾。

地球，我的母亲！
我想那缥缈的天球，是你化妆的明镜，
那昼间的太阳，夜间的太阴，
只不过是那明镜中的你自己的虚影。

地球，我的母亲！
我想那天空中一切的星球，
只不过是我们生物的眼球的虚影；
我只相信你是实有性的证明。

above,
a certain Father exists.

O earth, my mother,
I think everything in this world are incarnations
   of your body:
thunder is the breath of your might,
snow and rain the upsurge of your blood.

O earth, my mother,
I think that the lofty bowl of the sky is the mirror in which you adorn yourself,
and that the sun by day and the moon by night
are but your reflections in the mirror.

O earth, my mother,
I think all the stars in the sky
are but the eyes of us your creatures reflected
   in the mirror.
I can only think you are the witness to the reality of existence.

地球,我的母亲!
已往的我,只是个知识未开的婴孩,
我只知道贪受着你的深恩,
我不知道你的深恩,不知道报答你的深恩。

地球,我的母亲!
从今后我知道你的深恩,
我饮一杯水,纵是天降的甘霖,
我知道那是你的乳,我的生命羹。

地球,我的母亲!
我听着一切的声音言笑,
我知道那是你的歌,
特为安慰我的灵魂。

地球,我的母亲!
我眼前一切的浮游生动,
我知道那是你的舞,
特为安慰我的灵魂。

O earth, my mother,
my former self was just an ignorant child,
I only enjoyed your affection,
I did not understand, I did not know how to repay your affection.

O earth, my mother,
henceforth I shall realize how loving you are;
if I drink a glass of water, even if it is from
   Heaven-sent dew,
I shall know it is your milk, my life-sustaining
   drink.

O earth, my mother,
whenever I hear a voice speak or laugh
I know it is your song,
expressly provided to comfort my spirit.

O earth, my mother,
before my eyes everything is in restless motion;
I know this is your dance
with which you wish to comfort my soul.

地球，我的母亲！
我感觉着一切的芬芳彩色，
我知道那是你给我的玩品，
特为安慰我的灵魂。

地球，我的母亲！
我的灵魂便是你的灵魂，
我要强健我的灵魂，
用来报答你的深恩。

地球，我的母亲！
从今后我要报答你的深恩，
我知道你爱我还要劳我，
我要学着你劳动，永久不停！

1919 年 12 月末作

O earth, my mother,
I savour every fragrance, every colour;
I know they are palythings you have given me
expressly to comfort my spirit.

O earth, my mother,
my spirit is your spirit;
I shall make my spirit strong
to repay your affection.

O earth, my mother,
henceforth I shall repay your affection;
I know that you love me and wish to encourage
  me to work,
I shall learn from you to work, never to stop.

December 1919

雪　朝

——读 Carlyle：“The Hero as Poet”的时候

雪的波涛！
一个银白的宇宙！
我全身心好像要化为了光明流去，
Open – secret 哟！

楼头的檐溜……
那可不是我全身的血液？
我全身的血液点滴出律吕的幽音，
同那海涛相和，松涛相和，雪涛相和。

哦哦！大自然的雄浑哟！
大自然的 *symphony* 哟！
Hero – poet 哟！
Proletarian poet 哟！

1919 年 12 月作

Morning Snow

– On reading Carlyle's The Hero as Poet

Waves of snow.
A world all of silver.
My whole being is ready to resolve into light
   and flow forth,
an open secret.

Water dripping from the eaves....
Surely it is my life's blood?
My life's blood drips with muted cadence,
in harmony with the waves of the sea, of the
   pines, of the snow.

Nature, how bold your sweep.
The symphony that is Nature.
Hero-poet.
Proletarian poet.

December 1919

光　海

无限的大自然，
成了一个光海了。
到处都是生命的光波，
到处都是新鲜的情调，
到处都是诗，
到处都是笑：
海也在笑，
山也在笑，
太阳也在笑，
地球也在笑，
我同阿和，我的嫩苗，
同在笑中笑。

翡翠一样的青松，
笑着在把我们手招。
银箔一样的沙原，
笑着待把我们拥抱。
我们来了。

Sea of Light

Unbounded Nature
has become a sea of light.
Everywhere is life in pulsing light-waves,
everywhere a new spirit in the air,
everywhere poetry,
everywhere laughter:
a laughing sea
and laughing hills,
a laughing sun
and a laughing earth,
while I and Ah-ho, my tender shoot,
laugh together in this world of laughter.

Emerald-green, a fir-tree
beckons us with a smile.
The sands, a sheet of silver leaf,
invite us laughing to their embrace.
We are here!

你快拥抱！
我们要在你怀儿的当中，
洗个光之澡！

一群小学的儿童，
正在沙中跳跃。
你撒一把沙，
我还一声笑；
你又把我推翻，
我反把你揎倒。
我回到十五年前的旧我了。

十五年前的旧我呀，
也还是这么年少，
我住在青衣江上的嘉州，
我住在至乐山下的高小。
至乐山下的母校呀！
你怀儿中的沙场，我的摇篮，
可还是这么光耀？
唉！我有个心爱的同窗，
听说今年死了！

Hug us, then!
And in your bosom we shall bathe in light.

Acrowd of school-children
are skipping about in the sand:
one throws a handful of sand,
another laughs back at him;
the first pushes the second one over,
the other one sends the first sprawling.
I am back in my boyhood of fifteen years ago.

Fifteen years ago
I was a boy like you.
I lived at Kiachow on the River Chingyi,
at the school nestling at the foot of Mount
    Chihlo.
The school that nurtured me!
The sandy yard where I played within your
    care—
does it still glow with its old radiance?
Ah, I had a favourite school-friend then,
I heard, alas, he died this year.

我契己的心友呀！
你蒲柳一样的风姿，
还在我眼底留连，
你解放了的灵魂，
可也在我身旁欢笑？
你灵肉解体的时分，
念到你海外的知交，
你流了眼泪多少？……

哦，那个玲珑的石造的灯台，
正在海上光照，
阿和要我登，
我们登上了。
哦，山在那儿燃烧，
银在波中舞蹈，
一只只的帆船，
好像是在镜中跑，
哦，白云也在镜中跑，
这不是个呀，生命底写照！

阿和，哪儿是青天？

Comrade sworn to lasting friendship.
Fragile as the early willow,
your form still lingers before my eyes.
Could your liberated spirit
still be happily laughing at my side?
When, at the parting of flesh and spirit,
you remembered your friend beyond the seas,
how many tears did you shed for him? . . .

Oh, that trim little stone lighthouse
shining out over the sea.
Ah-ho wants me to go up it;
we climb up.
The hills are on fire,
silver dances on the waves,
a line of sailing – boats
seem to be slipping by in a mirror,
so seem the clouds to slip by;
and this—why, it is the image of life itself.

Ah-ho, where is the blue sky?

他指着头上的苍昊。
阿和，哪儿是大地？
他指着海中的洲岛。
阿和，哪儿是爹爹？
他指着空中的一只飞鸟。
哦哈，我便是那只飞鸟！
我便是那只飞鸟！
我要同白云比飞，
我要同明帆赛跑。
你看我们哪个飞得高？
你看我们哪个跑得好？

He points to the azure expanse overhead.
Ah-ho, where is the earth?
He points to the islands in the sea.
Ah-ho, where is Daddy?
He points to a bird flying in the air.
Aha! So I am that flying bird!
I am that flying bird!
Watch me outfly the white clouds,
watch me race against the gleaming sails,
and see who flies the higher,
see who speeds the faster.

梅花树下醉歌

——游日本太宰府

梅花！梅花！
我赞美你！我赞美你！
你从你自我当中
吐露出清淡的天香，
开放出窈窕的好花。
花呀！爱呀！
宇宙的精髓呀！
生命的泉水呀！
假使春天没有花，
人生没有爱，
到底成了个什么世界？
梅花呀！梅花呀！
我赞美你！
我赞美我自己！
我赞美这自我表现的全宇宙的本体！

Drunken Song Under
a Flowering Plum Tree

– Travelling in Dazaifu in Japan

Plum tree! Plum tree!
I sing your praises! I sing your praises!
You from your innermost self
exhale your faint unearthly fragrance
and put forth your lovely flowers.
Flowers! Love!
Quintessence of the universe,
source of life!
Were spring without flowers,
life without love,
what kind of a world would it be?
Plum blossom! Plum blossom!
I sing your praises,
I sing the praises of myself,
I sing the praises of the self-expressive uni-
    verse.

还有什么你？
还有什么我？
还有什么古人？
还有什么异邦的名所？
一切的偶像都在我面前毁破！
破！破！破！
我要把我的声带唱破！

Is there really a you?

Is there really a me?

Is there really an antiquity?

Are there really famous places in foreign
  climes?

Every idol has been struck down before me!

Down! Down! Down! I would snap my vocal
  chords in song!

夜步十里松原

海已安眠了。
远望去,只看见白茫茫一片幽光,
听不出丝毫的涛声波语。
哦,太空! 怎么那样地高超,自由,雄浑,清寥!
无数的明星正圆睁着他们的眼儿,
在眺望这美丽的夜景。
十里松原中无数的古松,
都高擎着他们的手儿沉默着在赞美天宇。
他们一枝枝的手儿在空中战栗,
我的一枝枝的神经纤维在身中战栗。

Pacing Through Jurimatsubara
at Night

The ocean sleeps in peace.
Gaze into the distance, only a misty glow can
    be seen,
not the faintest murmur of waves can be heard.
Ah, you spacious heavens, how lofty you are,
    how free, how mighty, how vast and se-
    renet!
Countless stars look down wide-eyed,
their gaze fixed on the beauty of the night.
Countless pines in Jurimatsubara
raise high their hands in silent adoration of the
    heavens;
their hands tremble in awe against the sky;
every fibre of my nerves trembles in awe within
    me!

我是个偶像崇拜者

我是个偶像崇拜者呦！
我崇拜太阳，崇拜山岳，崇拜海洋；
我崇拜水，崇拜火，崇拜火山，崇拜伟大的江河；
我崇拜生，崇拜死，崇拜光明，崇拜黑夜；
我崇拜苏彝士、巴拿马、万里长城、金字塔，
我崇拜创造的精神，崇拜力，崇拜血，崇拜心脏；
我崇拜炸弹，崇拜悲哀，崇拜破坏；
我崇拜偶像破坏者，崇拜我！
我又是个偶像破坏者呦！

1920 年 5、6 月间作

114

I Am an Idolater

I am an idolater;
I worship the sun, worship mountain peaks,
  worship the sea;
I worship water, worship fire, worship volca-
  noes, worship the great rivers;
I worship life, worship death, worship light,
  worship darkness;
I worship Suez, worship Panama, worship the
  Great Wall, worship the Pyramids;
I worship the creative spirit, worship strength,
  worship blood, worship the heart;
I worship bombs, worship sorrow, worship de-
  struction;
I worship iconoclasts, worship myself,
  for I am also an iconoclast!

May – June 1920

115

太阳礼赞

青沉沉的大海,波涛汹涌着,潮向东方。
光芒万丈地,将要出现了哟——新生的太阳!

天海中的云岛都已笑得来火一样地鲜明!
我恨不得,把我眼前的障碍一概划平!

出现了哟! 出现了哟! 耿晶晶地白灼的圆光!
从我两眸中有无限道的金丝向着太阳飞放。

太阳哟! 我背立在大海边头紧觑着你。
太阳哟! 你不把我照得个通明,我不回去!

Hymn to the Sun

Glaucous ocean, clamorous breakers, eastward-
   running tide,
with immense glow soon will emerge the new-
   born sun.

Cloud-islands in the sea of the sky are fire-fresh
   and smiling.
Oh, if only I could level every obstacle to my
   view.

There it comes! There it comes! Crystal white
   circlet:
endless golden threads fly from my pupils to the
   sun.

Sun! Standing on the water's edge, my back to
   the land, I fix my gaze on you.
Sun! Until you have pervaded me with your

太阳哟！你请永远照在我的面前，不使退转！

太阳哟！我眼光背开了你时，四面都是黑暗！

太阳哟！你请把我全部的生命照成道鲜红的血流！

太阳哟！你请把我全部的诗歌照成些金色的浮沤！

太阳哟！我心海中的云岛也已笑得来火一样地鲜明了！

太阳哟！你请永远倾听着，倾听着，我心海中的怒涛！

light I shall not turn away.

Sun! Shine on me for ever, do not turn away.
Sun! When I remove my eyes from you, all
round me is darkness.

Sun! Make my entire life a flow of fresh
blood.
Sun! Turn all my poems into a golden foam.

Sun! The cloud-islands in the sea of my heart
are fire-fresh and smiling.
Sun! Hearken ever to the angry surge of my
heart.

沙上的脚印

一

太阳照在我右方，
把我全身的影儿
投在了左边的海里；
沙岸上留了我许多的脚印。

二

太阳照在我左方，
把我全身的影儿
投在了右边的海里；
沙岸上留了我许多的脚印。

三

太阳照在我后方，
把我全身的影儿

Footprints in the Sand

I

The sun shines from my right,
casts the full shadow of my body
on the sea to my left.
The sandy beach holds many footprints of
  mine.

II

The sun shines from my left,
casts the full shadow of my body
on the sea to my right.
The sandy beach holds many footprints of
  mine.

III

The sun shines at my back,
casts the full shadow of my body

投在了前边的海里；
海潮哟，别要荡去了沙上的脚印！

四

太阳照在我前方，
太阳哟！可也曾把我全身的影儿
投在了后边的海里？
哦，海潮儿早已荡去了沙上的脚印！

122

on the sea in front of me.
Do not, O sea, scour away my prints from the
  sand!

IV

The sun shines in front of me.
Sun, have you cast my full shadow
on the sea at my back?
Ah, the tide has long since washed away the
  footprints in the sand!

金字塔

其一

一个,两个,三个,三个金字塔的尖端
排列在尼罗河畔——是否是尼罗河畔?——
一个高,一个低,一个最低,
塔下的河岸刀截断了一样地整齐,
哦,河中流泻着的涟漪哟!塔后汹涌着的云霞
　　哟!
云霞中隐约地一团白光,恐怕是将要西下的太
　　阳。
太阳游历了地球东半,又要去游历地球西半,
地球上的天工人美怕全盘都已被你看完!
否,否,不然!是地球在自转,公转,

Pyramids

I

First one, then two, then three pyramid peaks
range on the banks of the Nile—are these not
   the Nile banks?
One high, one lower, the last lowest of all.
The river banks below run on neat as a knife
   cut.
Ah, those ripples in the river's flow, those rosy
   clouds surging behind the pyramids!
A white blur of light shows through the clouds:
   it must be the westering sun;
the sun has traversed the eastern hemisphere, it
   will now visit the western.
The natural and man-made beauties must all
   have passed before your gaze.
No! No! Not So! It is the earth that is turning
   and circling you

就好像一个跳舞着的女郎将就你看。
太阳哟！太阳的象征哟！金字塔哟！
我恨不能飞随你去哟！飞向你去哟！

其二

左右蓊郁着两列森林，
中间流泻着一个反写的"之"字，
流向那晚霞重叠的金字塔底。
伟大的寂寥哟，死的沉默哟，
我凝视着，倾听着……
三个金字塔的尖端
好像同时有宏朗的声音在吐：
创造哟！创造哟！努力创造哟！
人们创造力的权威可与神祇比伍！
不信请看我，看我这雄伟的巨制吧！
便是天上的太阳也在向我低头呀！
哦哦，渊默的雷声！我感谢你现身的说教！

like a dancing girl approaching you.
Sun! Symbol of the sun! Pyramids!
Oh, that I might follow you in your course, fly
    towards you!

II

On either side runs a line of sombre woods:
between them flows a Z-shaped ribbon,
flowing towards the foot of the cloud-lapped
    pyramids.
Majestic solitude, deathly silence. . . .
The points of all three pyramids
seem at the same time to be proclaiming in so-
    norous voices:
Create! Create! Create with all your might!
The creative forces of man can rival those of
    the gods.
If you will not believe, look upon us, we grandi-
    ose structures!
Even the sun in the sky must bow his head to
    us!
Sonorous thunder, I am grateful for this your

我心海中的情涛也已流成了个河流流向你了！
森林中流泻着的"之"江可不是我吗？

1920 年 6、7 月间作

self-tested advice.
The surging feelings in the sea of my heart have
    converged into a river that flows towards
    you.
Surely that Z-shaped river in the woods must be
    me myself!

June-July 1920

胜利的死

爱尔兰独立军领袖，新芬党员马克司威尼，自八月中旬为英政府所逮捕以来，幽囚于剥里克士通监狱中，耻不食英粟者七十有三日，终以一千九百二十年十月二十五日死于狱。

其一

Oh! once again to Freedom's cause return,
The patriot Tell – the Bruce of Bannock – burn!
爱国者兑尔——邦诺克白村的布鲁士，
哦，请为自由之故而再生！

—Thomas Campbell

哦哦！这是张"眼泪之海"的写真呀！
森严阴耸的大厦——可是监狱的门前？可是礼
　拜堂的外面？
一群不可数尽的儿童正在跪着祈祷呀！

"爱尔兰独立军的领袖马克司威尼，

Victorious in Death

(Terence MacSwiney, the Sinn Feiner, a leader of the Irish Republican Army, was arrested by the British Government in the middle of August 1920 and imprisoned in Parkstone Jail. For seventy-three days he disdained to eat the English bread and died there on October 25.)

I

Oh! Once again to Freedom's cause return,
The patriot Tell— the Bruce of Bannockburn!
True depiction of "the sea of tears,"
gaunt forbidding pile: can it be the gateway to a
　　prison, or the outside of a church?
Acountless throng of young men kneel at
　　prayer.

"MacSwiney, leader of the Irish Republican Ar-
　　my,

投在英格兰,剥里克士通监狱中已经五十余日
　　了,
入狱以来耻不食英粟;
爱尔兰的儿童——跪在大厦前面的儿童
感谢他爱国的至诚,
正在为他请求加护,祈祷。"

可敬的马克司威尼呀!
可爱的爱尔兰的儿童呀!
自由之神终会要加护你们,
因为你们能自相加护,
因为你们是自由神的化身故!

　　　　　　　　　　　　　10 月 13 日

其二

Hope, for a for season, bade the world farewell,
And Freedom shrieked – as Kasciusko fell!
希望,暂时向世界告别了,
自由也发出惊叫——当珂斯修士哥死了!
　　　　　　　　　　　　——Thomas Campbell

爱尔兰的志士! 马克司威尼!
今天是十月二十二日了!(我壁上的日历永不

cast into Parkstone Gaol fifty days ago and
    more,
has spurned ever since the shameful English
    bread.
We sons of Ireland, kneeling before this great
    building,
are deeply moved by his devotion.
We offer up our prayers for his protection."

Honoured MacSwiney!
Dear sons of Ireland,
the spirit of freedom will ever stand by you,
for you stand by one another,
you are the incarnation of freedom!

October 13

II

Hope, for a season, bade the world farwell,
And Freedom shrieked—as Kosciusko fell!
Terence MacSwiney, Irish patriot!
Today is the 22nd of October!

曾引我如此注意）

你因在剥里克士通监狱中可还活着在吗？

十月十七日伦敦发来的电信

说你断食以来已经六十六日了，

然而容态依然良好；

说你十七日的午后还和你的亲人对谈了须臾，

然而你的神采比从前更加光辉；

说你身体虽日渐衰颓，

然而今天是十月二十二日了！

爱尔兰的志士！马克司威尼呀！

此时此刻的有机物汇当中可还有你的生命存在
吗？

十月十七日你的故乡——可尔克市——发来的
电信

说是你的同志新芬党员之一人，匪持谢乐德，

因在可尔克市监狱中断食以来已六十有八日，

终以十七日之黄昏溘然长逝了。

——啊！有史以来罕曾有的哀烈的惨死呀！

(Never has the calendar on the wall so fixed
    my attention!)
Are you still alive, locked in your prison cell?
Came a cable of the 17th from London:
It was sixty-six days since your fast began,
and yet you bear yourself as well as ever.
You talked for a while with your dear ones on
    the afternoon of the 17th,
and your face was even more radiant than be-
    fore.
Your strength was failing daily...
and today is the 22nd of October.
Irish patriot, Terence MacSwiney!
Can you still be counted among living crea-
    tures?
A cable of the 17th from your native Cork
told that a Sinn Feiner, comrade of yours,
    Fitzgerald,
fasted for sixty-eight days in Cork City Gaol,
and suddenly died at sundown on the 17th.
Cruel deaths there are in history, but few so
    tragic.

爱尔兰的首阳山！爱尔兰的伯夷，叔齐哟！
我怕读得今日以后再来的电信了！

· 10 月 22 日

其三

Oh！ sacred Truth！ thy triumph ceased a while，
And Hope，thy sister，ceased with thee to smile.
哦，神圣的真理！你的胜利暂停了一忽，
你的姊妹，希望，也同你一道停止了微笑。

——Thomas Campbell

十月二十一日伦敦发来的电信又到了！
说是马克司威尼已经昏死了去三回了！
说是他的妹子向他的友人打了个电报：
望可尔克的市民早为她的哥哥祈祷，
祈祷他早一刻死亡，少一刻痛伤！
不忍卒读的伤心人语哟！读了这句话的人有不
流眼泪的吗？
猛兽一样的杀人政府哟！你总要在世界史中添
出一个永远不能磨灭的污点！

The Shouyang Mountain of Ireland! The Po-yi
and Shu-chi of Ireland!
The next cable I dread to read...

October 22

III

O sacred Truth! Thy triumph ceased a while,
And Hope, thy sister, ceased with thee to
smile.
Now arrives a cable of the 21st:
Three times MacSwiney has fainted.
His sister has sent a telegram to his friends,
hoping that the citizens have offered prayers for
her brother.
She prays that he may die the sooner, and his
agony be ended.
Who could bear to read to the end these heart-
breaking words?
Who could restrain his tears?
Bestial murderous government, are you bent on
casting an in-delible stain on the history of
the world?

冷酷如铁的英人们呀！你们的血管之中早没有
　　拜伦、康沫尔的血液循环了吗？
你暗淡无光的月轮哟！我希望我们这阴莽莽的
　　地球，就在这一刹那间，早早同你一样冰化！

10 月 24 日

其四

Truth shall restore the light by Nature given,
And, like Prometheus, bring the fire of Heaven!
真理，你将恢复自然所给予的光，
如像普罗美修士带来天火一样！

——Thomas Campbell

汪洋的大海正在唱着他悲壮的哀歌，
穹窿无际的青天已经哭红了他的脸面，
远远的西方，太阳沉没了！——
悲壮的死哟！金光灿烂的死哟！凯旋同等的死
　　哟！
胜利的死哟！
兼爱无私的死神！我感谢你哟！你把我敬爱无
　　暨的马克司威尼早早救了！
自由的战士，马克司威尼，你表示出我们人类意
　　志的权威如此伟大！

Cruel, callous Englishmen, has the blood of Byron and Camp-bell ceased to flow in your
veins?
Lustreless moon, would that our sombre earth
might on the instant be turned like you to ice!

October 24

IV

Truth shall restore the light by Nature given,
And, like Prometheus, bring the fire of Heav-
en!
The mighty ocean is sobbing its sad lament,
the boundless abyss of the sky is red with
weeping,
far, far away the sun has sunk in the west.
Brave, tragic death! Death in a blaze of glory!
Triumphal procession of a victor! Victorious death!
Impartial God of Death! I am grateful to you!
You have saved the MacSwiney for whom my love
and reverence know no bounds!
MacSwiney, fighter for freedom, you have

我感谢你呀！赞美你呀！"自由"从此不死了！
　夜幕闭了后的月轮哟！何等光明呀！……

10 月 27 日

〔附白〕这四节诗是我数日间热泪的结晶体。各节弁首的诗句都是从苏格兰诗人康沫尔(Thomas Campbell, 1777 – 1844)二十二岁时所作《哀波兰》(The Downfall of Poland)一诗引出,此诗余以为可与拜伦的《哀希腊》一诗并读。拜伦助希腊独立,不得志而病死;康氏亦屡捐献资金以惠助波兰,两诗人义侠之气亦差堪伯仲。如今希腊、波兰均已更生,而拜伦、康沫尔均已逝世;然而西方有第二之波兰,东方有第二之希腊,我希望拜伦、康沫尔之精神"Once again to Freedom's cause return!"(请为自由之故而再生!)

140

shown how great can be the power of the human
will!

    I am grateful to you, I extol you; freedom can
        henceforth never die!
    The night has closed down on us, but how
        bright is the moon...

October 27

    In these four stanzas were crystallized the hot tears shed
by me during those days. At the head of each stanza are lines
quoted from the Downfall of Poland of the Scottish poet, Thomas Campbell (1777 – 1844). They may be read in conjunction
with "The Glory That Was Greece" formDon Juan, and "Fair
Greece! Sad Relic" from Childe Harold of Byron. Byron fought
for an independent Greece; the struggle ended in defeat in
which Byron died. Campbell gave money many times to aid
Poland. The two poets rival each other in nobility of spirit. Poland and Greece are now reborn, and Byron and Campbell are
no longer living, but there is a second Poland in the West and
a second Greece in the East. May the spirit of Byron and
Campbell "Once again to Freedom's cause return"!

Venus

我把你这张爱嘴，
比成着一个酒杯。
喝不尽的葡萄美酒，
会使我时常沉醉！

我把你这对乳头，
比成着两座坟墓。
我们俩睡在墓中，
血液儿化成甘露！

1919 年间作

Venus

I would compare your enchanting lips
to a wine-cup.
I would be intoxicated time without number
from its inexhaustible nectar.

I would compare your breasts
to two grave mounds.
Were we two to sleep in these graves
our blood would change to sweet dew.

1919

别　离

残月黄金梳，
我欲掇之赠彼姝。
彼姝不可见，
桥下流泉声如泫。

晓日月桂冠，
掇之欲上青天难。
青天犹可上，
生离令我情惆怅。

〔附白〕此诗内容余曾改译如下：
一弯残月儿
　　还高挂在天上。
一轮红日儿
　　早已出自东方。
我送了她回来，
　　走到这旭川桥上；
应着桥下流水的哀音，
　　我的灵魂儿
　　向我这般歌唱：
月儿啊！
　　你同那黄金梳儿一样。
我要想爬上天去，
　　把你取来；
用着我的手儿，
　　插在她的头上。
咳！
　　天这样的高，

144

Parting

The curved arc of the waning moon
hangs yet in the sky.
The red disc of the sun
has long emerged from the east.
I went to see her off,
went on the bridge over Asahigawa River.
The current below sang its sad song.
My soul responded,
snag to me this song:

Moon!
You are like a golden comb.
I would like to climb up to the sky,
pluck you down,
and with my hand
I would set you in her hair.
Oh my dear!
The sky is so far away,

我怎能爬得上?
　天这样的高,
　我纵能爬得上,
我的爱呀!
　你今儿到了哪方?

太阳呀!
　你同那月桂冠儿一样。
　我要想爬上天去,
　把你取来;
　借着她的手儿,
　戴在我的头上。
咳!
　天这样的高,
　我怎能爬得上?
　天这样的高,
　我纵能爬得上,
我的爱呀!
　你今儿到了哪方?

一弯残月儿
　还高挂在天上。
一轮红日儿
　早已出自东方。
我送了她回来
走到旭川桥上;

how could I climb up there?
Then sky is so far away,
but even if I could climb up there,
O, my love,
where are you now?

Sun!
You are laurels for a poet.
I would like to climb up to the sky,
to take hold of you,
and with her hands
place you on my head.
O, my dear!
The sky is so far away,
how could I ever climb up there?
The sky is so far away,
but even if I could climb up there,
O, my love,
where are you now?

The curved arc of the waning moon
hangs yet in the sky.
The red disc of the sun
has long emerged from the east.
I went to see her off,
went on the birdge over Asahigawa River

应着桥下流水的哀音，
　我的灵魂儿
　向我这般歌唱。

1919 年 3、4 月间作

148

The current below sang its sad song.
My soul responded,
snag to me this song.

March – April 1919

春　愁

是我意凄迷？

是天萧条耶？

如何春日光，

惨淡无明辉？

如何彼岸山，

低头不展眉？

周遭打岸声，

海兮汝语谁？

海语终难解，

空见白云飞。

1919 年 3、4 月间作

150

Spring Sadness

Is it that melancholy is clouding my mind?
Or is it the desolate bleakness of the sky?
How is it that the spring sunlight
is so drear and bereft of brilliance?
Why do the hills on yonder shore
bow their beads in frowning dejection?
The air is filled with the beat of the waves on
    the shore.
O sea! to whom are you speaking?
But I can make nothing of the words of the
    sea,
for me the flight of the white clouds has no
    meaning.

                        March – April 1919

新月与白云

月儿呀！你好像把镀金的镰刀。
你把这海上的松树斫倒了，
哦，我也被你斫倒了！

白云呀！你是不是解渴的凌冰？
我怎得把你吞下喉去，
解解我火一样的焦心？

1919 年夏秋之间作

New Moon and White Clouds

Moon! You are like a gilded sickle.
You have felled the fir-trees on this sea,
yes, and I too have been felled by you!

White clouds! Are you, I wonder, cool ice to
   slake the thirst?
Oh that I could swallow you down my throat
and quench the fires that rage in my breast!

Written between summer and autumn, 1919

鹭鸶

鹭鸶！鹭鸶！

你自从哪儿飞来？

你要向哪儿飞去？

你在空中画了一个椭圆，

突然飞下海里，

你又飞向空中去。

你突然又飞下海里，

你又飞向空中去。

雪白的鹭鸶！

你到底要飞向哪儿去？

1919 年夏秋之间作

154

Egret

Egret! Egret!
Where have you flown from,
where are you flying to?
You describe an ellipse against the sky,
then in an instant you swoop down to the sea.
Again you fly up into the sky,
then again you swoop down to the sea,
yet again you fly up into mid-air.
Snowy-white egret!
Where can you be flying to?

Written between summer and autumn, 1919

春　蚕

蚕儿呀,你在吐丝……
哦,你在吐诗!
你的诗,怎么那样地
纤细、明媚、柔腻、纯粹!
那样地……嗳!我已形容不出你。

蚕儿呀,你的诗
可还是出于有心?无意?
造作矫揉?自然流泻?
你可是为的他人?
还是为的你自己?

蚕儿呀,我想你的诗
终怕是出于无心,
终怕是出于自然流泻。
你在创造你的"艺术之宫",
终怕是为的你自己。

Spring Silkworms

Silkworms, you are spinning silk....
No, it is poetry you are spinning!
How gossamer your poetry, how charming, how
  delicate, how pure, how sparkling,
how very...why I can find no words to describe you!

Silkworms, your poetry—
is it premeditated or unprompted?
Do you create with art, or is it a natural flow?
Do you make it for others,
or for yourselves alone?

Silkworms, I am afraid that your poetry
is, alas, spontaneous,
is, alas, a natural flow.
The Palace of Art you are erecting,
is, alas, for yourselves alone.

蜜桑索罗普之夜歌

无边天海呀！
一个水银的浮沤！
上有星汉湛波，
下有融晶泛流，
正是有生之伦睡眠时候。
我独披着件白孔雀的羽衣，
遥遥地，遥遥地，
在一只象牙舟上翘首。

啊，我与其学做个泪珠的鲛人，
返向那沉黑的海底流泪偷生，
宁在这缥缈的银辉之中，
就好像那个坠落了的星辰，
曳着带幻灭的美光，
向着"无穷"长殒！
前进！……前进！
莫辜负了前面的那轮月明！

1920 年 11 月 23 日

158

Night Song of a Misanthropist

Boundless sea of the sky!
Quicksilver bubble!
Above, the clear flow of the River of Stars,
below, the molten crystal of the surge.
Now is the time when all living things sleep.
Alone, cloaked in the plumes of the white pea-
    cock,
far away, far away fleeting,
I raise my head in an ivory skiff.
Not for me to ape the chiao jen, weeping pearls
    for tears,
to return to the sombre depths and by these
    tears eke out a life.
No! Rather in this dim silvery radiance,
like the fallen star,
trail my evanescent glory,
plunge deep down to "Eternity."
Forward!...Forward!
Let me not disappoint the moon before me!

November 23, 1920

霁 月

淡淡地，幽光
浸洗着海上的森林。
森林中寥寂深深，
还滴着黄昏时分的新雨。

云母面就了般的白杨行道
坦坦地在我面前导引，
引我向沉默的海边徐行。
一阵阵的暗香和我亲吻。

我身上觉着轻寒，
你偏那样地云衣重裹，
你团栾无缺的明月哟，
请借件缟素的衣裳给我。

我眼中莫有睡眠，
你偏那样地雾帷深锁。
你渊默无声的银海哟，
请提起幽渺的波音和我。

Moonlight After Rain

Wanly your glimmer
bathes the woods by the sea;
the lonely depths of the woods
drip still with the fresh rain of twilight.

Pearly face of the poplar avenue,
you lead onwards before me in your level
   sweep,
guide me to the silent shore;
wafts of secret fragrance caress me.

A slight chill comes over me:
you wrapped in those layers of cloudy raiment,
you, whose sphere is faultlessly round,
lend me, I pray you, of your pure silk garments.

I have no sleep in my eyes:
you who delight to swathe yourself in misty
   draperies,
you silent abysmal silver ocean,
attune to me the secret music of your waves.

晴　朝

池上几株新柳，
柳下一座长亭，
亭中坐着我和儿，
池中映着日和云。

鸡声、群鸟声、鹦鹉声，
溶流着的水晶一样！
粉蝶儿飞去飞来，
泥燕儿飞来飞往。

落叶蹁跹，
飞下池中水。
绿叶蹁跹，
翻弄空中银辉。

一只白鸟
来在池中飞舞。
哦，一湾的碎玉！
无限的青蒲！

Bright Morning

Over the pool are young willows,
under the willows a long shelter;
in the shelter are seated my son and I.
On the pool are reflected sun and clouds.

Cockcrow, bird-call, parrot-screech
run on like a crystal stream;
butterflies flutter hither and thither,
the mud swallow darts hither and thither.

Dead leaves lurch as they fall,
float down into the pool;
green leaves swing in the air,
give off a silvery gleam above us.

A white bird
dances into the centre of the pool:
ah, a whole lagoon of splintered jade!
Unending rushbeds beyond.

岸　上

其　一

岸上的微风
早已这么清和！
远远的海天之交，
只剩着晚红一线。
海水渊青，
沉默着断绝声哗。
青青的郊原中，
慢慢地移着步儿，
只惊得草里的虾蟆四窜。
渔家处处，
吐放着朵朵有凉意的圆光。
一轮皓月儿
早在那天心孤照。
我吹着支
小小的哈牟尼笳，
坐在这海岸边的破船板上。
一种寥寂的幽音
好像要充满那些莹洁的寰空。

164

On the Shore

I

The breeze on the shore
already blows cool and mild;
the distant merging of sea and sky
is but a red trace of sunset.
The sea has emerald depths,
its deep silence cuts off all tumult from me.
In the green heathland
I move with slow footsteps:
alone the disturbed frogs scurry off.
Here and there are fishermen's cottages,
cool beads of light spring out from them.
A dazzling moon
shines down from the lonely depths of the sky.
Seated on a broken hulk on the shore
I play a small harmonica:
a plaintive melody
seems to fill the pure vault of the sky.

我的身心
好像是——融化着在。

1920 年 7 月 26 日

其二

天又昏黄了。
我独自一人
坐在这海岸上的渔舟里面，
我正对着那轮皓皓的月华，
深不可测的青空！
深不可测的天海呀！
海湾中喧阗着的涛声
猛烈地在我背后推荡！
Poseidon 呀，
你要把这只渔舟
替我推到那天海里去？

1920 年 7 月 27 日

其三

哦，火！
铅灰色的渔家顶上，

Body and soul are as though fused into one.

July 26, 1920

II

The sky is now growing dusky,
I remain a solitary figure,
I sit in the fishing-boat on the shore,
gazing upon the white radiance of the moon,
the unfathomable depths of the blue abyss
   above,
the unfathomable depths of the sea of the sky.
The clamorous waves in the bay
toss and churn savagely behind me.
Poseidon!
Could you not give a thrust to this boat for me,
and launch me on the sea of the sky?

July 27, 1920

III

The lead-grey roofs of the fishermen's cottages

昏昏的一团红火！
鲜红了……嫩红了……
橙黄了……金黄了……
依然还是那轮皓皓的月华！
"无穷世界的海边群儿相遇。
无际的青天静临，
不静的海水喧阗。
无穷世界的海边群儿相遇，叫着，跳着。"
我又坐在这破船板上，
我的阿和
和着一些孩儿们
同在沙中游戏。
我念着泰戈尔的一首诗，
我也去和着他们游戏。
嗳！我怎能成就个纯洁的孩儿？

1920 年 7 月 29 日

gleam darkly with a circle of red flame:

now crimson...now madder

now orange...now gold.

It is as ever the white radiance of the moon.

"On the seashore of endless worlds children
   meet.

The infinite sky is motionless overhead and the
   restless water is boisterous.

On the seashore of endless worlds the children
   meet with shouts and dances."

Again I sit on the broken hulk on the shore.

My little Ah-ho!

joins with a troop of children;

they play together on the sands.

Reciting this poem of Tagore

I go and play with them.

Ah! If only I could become a pure child!

July 29, 1920

晨　兴

月光一样的朝暾
照透了这蓊郁着的森林，
银白色的沙中交横着迷离的疏影。

松林外海水清澄，
远远的海中岛影昏昏，
好像是，还在恋着他昨宵的梦境。

携着个稚子徐行，
耳琴中交响着鸡声、鸟声，
我的心琴也微微地起了共鸣。

170

Stirrings of Morning

Morning, pale as moonlight,
penetrates the serried depths of the wood;
scattered shadows interlace confusedly on the
    silvery sand.

Clear the sea beyond the pines,
far, very far, shapes of islands loom hazily,
clinging still, one might think, to last night's
    dream.

Holding my boy by the hand, slowly I walk,
strings of my ears stir to the symphony of cock-
    crow, bird-call;
strings of my heart gently give off a sympathetic
    note.

春之胎动

独坐北窗下举目向楼外四望：
春在大自然的怀中胎动着在了！

远远一带海水呈着雌虹般的彩色，
俄而带紫，俄而深蓝，俄而嫩绿。

暗影与明辉在黄色的草原头交互浮动，
好像有探海灯在转换着的一般。

天空最高处作玉蓝色，有几朵白云飞驰；
白云的缘边色如乳糜，叫人微微眩目。

楼下一只白雄鸡，戴着鲜红的柔冠，

Stirrings of Spring

Seated alone by the north window I look all
  round.
In the womb of nature spring is stirring.

Far away the sea gleams with a faint irides-
  cence;
now it is purple, now deep blue, now a tender
  green.

Light and shade play on the yellow plain
as if swept by a searchlight.

The depths of the sky are a jade blue flecked
  with scudding clouds,
white clouds whose chyle-tinted edges almost
  dazzle the eye.

Down below I see a white cock with a soft

长长的声音叫得已有几分倦意了。

几只杂色的牝鸡偃伏在旁边的沙地中，
那些女郎们都带着些娇慵无力的样儿。
海上吹来的微风才在鸡尾上动摇，
早悄悄地偷来吻我的颜面，又偷跑了。

空漠处时而有小鸟的歌声。
几朵白云不知飞向何处去了。

海面上突然飞来一片白帆……
不一刹那间也不知飞向何处去了。

2 月 26 日

crimson comb.
Its long drawn-out call has now a note of tired
ness.

Some dappled hens are settled in the nearby
sand.
These young ladies have an air of languid indo-
lence.
The sea breeze is just enough to ruffle the
cock's tail.
It has already pressed the gentlest of stolen
kisses on my cheeks and away it steals.

From the lonely waste land comes intermittent
birdsong
and the white cloude have now sped away.

Suddenly a white sail comes sail comes into
view on the sea
and in a moment it, too, has sped away.

February 26

日暮的婚筵

夕阳,笼在蔷薇花色的纱罗中,
如像满月一轮,寂然有所思索。

恋着她的海水也故意装出个平静的样儿,
可他嫩绿的绢衣却遮不过他心中的激动。

几个十二三岁的小姑娘,笑语娟娟地,
在枯草原中替他们准备着结欢的婚筵。

新嫁娘最后涨红了她丰满的庞儿,
被她最心爱的情郎拥抱着去了。

2月28日

176

Wedding at Sundown

The setting sun, veiled in rose-tinted gauze,
is round as a full moon, silent and pensive.

The sea, too, that loves her, affects an outward
　calm,
but the pale green of his silks cannot hide the
　tumult in his heart.

Some delightful young girls, chattering and
　laughing,
prepare the joyful feast on the dry heathland.

At last the bride, her full cheeks flushed with
　crimson,
is take into her sweetheart's embrace.

February 28

海舟中望日出

铅的圆空，
　　蓝靛的大洋，
四望都无有，
　　只有动乱，荒凉，
黑汹汹的煤烟
　　恶魔一样！

云彩染了金黄，
　　还有一个爪痕露在天上。
那只黑色的海鸥
　　可要飞向何往？

我的心儿，好像
　　醉了一般模样。
我倚着船栏，
　　吐着胆浆……
哦！太阳！

Sunrise Seen from a Boat

Leaden circle of sky,
    indigo ocean,
an empty expanse meets the eye:
    only aimless movement, lonely wastes.
Black smoke bellying up
    like an evil demon.

The clouds are suffused with gold,
    there is a claw scratch in the sky.
See that black sea-bird,
    whither is it winging its way?

My heart might be
    a model for intoxication;
I stand at the rail
    and spit bile.

Sun!

白晶晶地一个圆珰！
在那海边天际
　黑云头上低昂。
那好容易才得盼见了你的容光！
　你请替我唱着凯旋歌哟！
我今朝可算是战胜了海洋！

4月3日

Rounded crystalline ear-ring
at the meeting of sky and sea,
you swing up and down over the black cloud.
It's not easy to get a glimpse of you.
Sing for me a triumphal ode.
All things considered, I've won my victory over the
sea today!

April 3

黄浦江口

平和之乡哟！
　我的父母之邦！
岸草那么青翠！
　流水这般嫩黄！

我倚着船栏远望，
　平坦的大地如像海洋，
除了一些青翠的柳波，
　全没有山崖阻障。

小舟在波上簸扬，
　人们如在梦中一样。
平和之乡哟！
　我的父母之邦！

4月3日

Estuary of the Whamoa

Peaceful village,
land of my fathers,
so green those grassy shores,
so straw-pale the flow of the water.

I lean on the rail and look into the distance:
level like an ocean is the great country,
but for a few heaving willows
not a hill or cliff hinders the view.

The little craft ride up and down,
the men might be in a dream.
Peaceful village,
land of my fathers.

April 3